BELAIR LESSON BANK

PSHE and Citizenship 1

Tina Rae

Contents

Introduction/Belair Lesson Banks on CD	3
All About Me	4
Feelings	8
Friends	12
Making Rules	16
My World and Your World — Groups	20
Responsible Jobs — People Who Help Us	24
My Body	28
Caring for Others	32
Solving Problems	36
Caring for Our Environments	40
Look to the Future	44
Useful Websites and Agencies	48

Belair Publications

First published in 2001 by Belair Publications.
United Kingdom: Belair Publications, Apex Business Centre, Boscombe Road, Dunstable LU5 4RL.
Email: belair@belair-publications.co.uk

Belair allows photocopying of pages marked 'copiable page' for educational use, providing that this use is within the confines of the purchasing institution. Copiable pages should not be declared in any return in respect of any photocopying licence.

© 2001 Belair Publications, on behalf of the author.

Belair books are protected by international copyright laws. All rights are reserved. The copyright of all materials in this book, except where otherwise stated, remains the property of the publisher and author. No part of this publication may be reproduced, stored in a retrieval system, or transmitted, in any form or by any means, for whatever purpose, without the written permission of Belair Publications.

Editor: Jennifer Steele
Layout artist: James Brown
Cover design: Martin Cross
Illustrations: Sue Woollatt (Graham-Cameron Illustration)

Every effort has been made to contact copyright holders of material used in this book. If any have been overlooked, we will be pleased to make any necessary arrangements.

British Library Cataloguing in Publication Data. A catalogue record for this book is available from the British Library.

Tina Rae hereby asserts her moral rights to be identified as the author of this work in accordance with the Copyright, Designs and Patents Act 1988.

ISBN 1 84191 093-7

Introduction

Personal, social and health education (PSHE) and citizenship should form an important part of every school curriculum, allowing for the development of essential social, emotional and life skills. These are the skills which are necessary in order to lead a confident and healthy life as a responsible and active citizen. This series of six books aims to provide resources for the PSHE and Citizenship curriculum, for children aged 5–11.

The basis of this series is to encourage children to:
- participate in a range of activities both within and outside of the existing curriculum and to make a distinct contribution to their own school and to the life of the community
- develop confidence, self-esteem and an awareness of their own worth as individuals, work co-operatively with others and develop the emotional awareness and empathy necessary to make and sustain positive relationships
- take on more responsibility – both for their own learning and for their own behaviour
- develop skills of reflection and gain an understanding of how they are developing as social beings
- confront and tackle a range of moral, social, spiritual and cultural issues that are all part of growing up
- consider political and social institutions and the rights and responsibilities of all individuals
- respect the diversity within their own communities.

There are 11 topics in each book, each with a teacher's page and three copiable activity pages. The teacher's page provides supporting notes, giving advice and information, and is organised as follows:

Introduction outlines the focus and philosophy of the chapter.
Learning Objectives outlines the skills on which each chapter focuses.
Discussion suggests points to be covered when first introducing the topic. It gives suggestions for both whole-class and group work.
Using the Activity Pages explains how to reinforce the learning in the pages.
Follow-up tasks provide further activity ideas, including creative work, written work, oral presentations and debates.

The activity pages are a photocopiable resource which can be completed in short time slots or extended into longer periods, depending on the length of time available. It is suggested that pupils are given the opportunity to work individually, in pairs or in small groups on the pages, giving plenty of opportunity to express their views and to listen actively to others.

Belair Lesson Banks on CD

All Belair *Lesson Banks* come in a CD format as well as book format. The CDs offer the children the opportunity to work on a computer, a learning tool they often find stimulating, while working through the same high-quality activities found in the book.

Key Features
- The discs have many activities on them including responding to pictures, writing frames, working in tables, sorting and matching activities.
- Many of the activities can be altered. If you, as the teacher, want to modify the language or change a question, you can do so easily. You can make changes such as:
  – simplify the text
  – add complexity to the language and structure
  – provide model answers or examples.
- Many screens have a linked screen which gives the children an opportunity to write an extended piece in response to a question.
- Finally, you can of course modify the activities on screen and print them out for the children to use as paper activities.

PDF Files for Lesson Bank CD-ROMS
Included on the CD-ROM is a folder containing all the pages from the book version (including the teacher's notes) in PDF format. To access these files, you will need a copy of Acrobat Reader.

Purchasers may copy this folder from the CD-ROM and store it on a single, non-networked computer without additional payment or need for a site licence. If the folder and its contents are stored on more than one computer or on a file server, then a site licence MUST be purchased. To obtain your site licence, write to N Carter at Belair Publications, Apex Business Centre, Boscombe Road, Dunstable LU5 4RL or email: NCarter@belair-publications.co.uk or fax 01582 475524. The site licence, of course, also gives you the right to use the CD-ROM on an unlimited number of computers within the purchasing institution.

ideas page

All About Me

Introduction

Being able to recognise and make the most of our skills and talents and beginning to learn from our mistakes and experiences are crucial skills which all children need to develop. They should be encouraged to reflect upon their own skills and experiences in order to recognise what they like and dislike and to distinguish between what is fair/unfair and what is right/wrong. It is vital that they are consequently given opportunities to share their ideas and views with others.

This topic requires children to reflect upon their appearance and family context, and to consider their personal likes and dislikes. It also asks them to articulate their own views and ideas, while at the same time developing an awareness of the beliefs and opinions of others in their peer group.

Learning Objectives

- To label their own physical characteristics and to recognise similarities and differences between themselves and others.
- To understand how they fit into their own family circle/context.
- To gain confidence in articulating their views and opinions.
- To recognise what they are good at and the importance of continually developing their skills.

Using the Activity Pages

My Appearance
Ensure that children have access to safety mirrors in order to look carefully at their own features. Encourage them to describe these features and start to develop an appropriate descriptive vocabulary. Highlight similarities and differences in the children's appearance and the importance of feeling and being happy with who you are. Children need to learn to identify and show respect for such differences.

My Family
Emphasise how families will be different and the importance of family members loving and caring for each other. Children need to be aware of the fact that they can show love, care and respect for those around them.

My Likes and Dislikes
Once the children have filled in this page, allow them to discuss their likes and dislikes with a friend, to see what the differences and similarities are. Allow each child to feed back their personal likes and dislikes to the rest of the class.

Discussion

In a circle time session ask all the children to identify three facts about themselves. Focus on positive points, such as things I like, things I can do well, people I love in my family, and factual information such as I am six years old, I am 1m 20cm. Make a 'we are good at' list, identifying the special qualities, skills and talents of all the children.

Identify the likes and dislikes of all the children in the class; for example, ask: What is your favourite food, game, activity, hobby, lesson? Generalise some opinions held by the whole class from these lists, such as we do not like people who hurt us, we like people in our families who love us, we like receiving presents.

Follow-up

- Reinforce the notion of having an identity – 'being me' – by reading relevant children's literature, such as *A Porcupine Named Fluffy* by Helen Lester.
- Make a 'Positive People' noticeboard displaying labelled photographs of all the children in the class supported by 'I can ...' cards. Each child can complete the sentence 'I can ...' in order to reinforce and highlight skills and strengths.
- Construct picture graphs/block graphs to illustrate what the children in the class like, such as favourite food, drink, game, TV programme.
- Make up 'My Family' books, drawing pictures of each member of the family on each page and completing the sentences: 'This is ...'; 'He/she can ...'.

My Appearance

- Draw your self-portrait inside the picture frame. Use a mirror and try to copy yourself.

This is me!

Name _____ date _____

- What colour are your eyes? _____
- What colour is your hair? _____
- What colour is your skin? _____

NOW Look at a friend's self-portrait. What are the differences?

My Family

- Who lives with you? Draw and label them in the family circle.

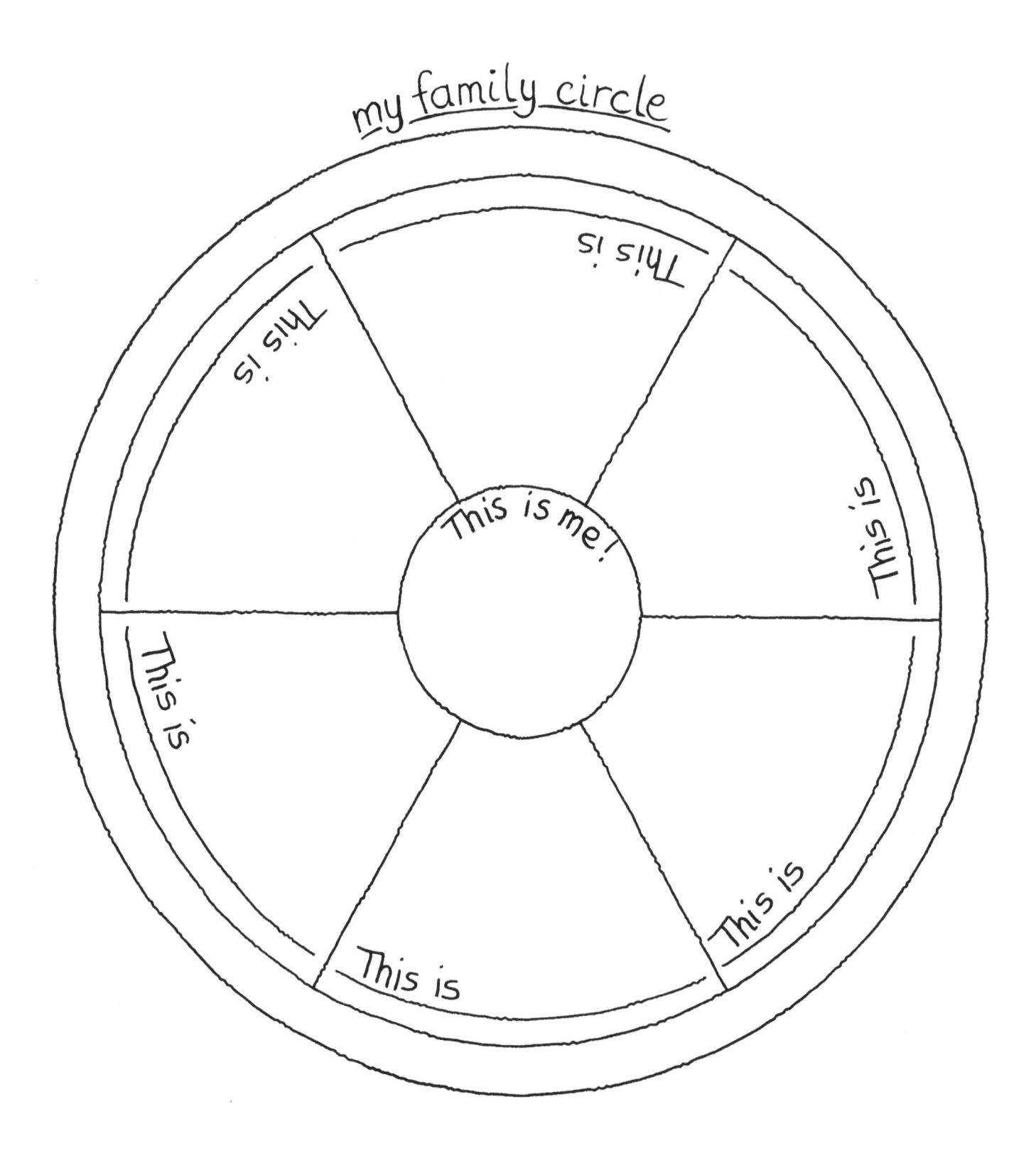

my family circle

This is me!

This is
This is
This is
This is
This is
This is

NOW Are there any more people in your family?
Write about the people in your family.

My Likes and Dislikes

- Write and draw the things that you like and do not like.

Likes	Dislikes
I like to eat _____.	I don't like to eat _____.
I like to play _____.	I don't like to play _____.
I like to help _____.	I don't like to help _____.
I like to wear _____.	I don't like to wear _____.

ideas page

Feelings

Introduction

Developing empathy and an understanding of other people's feelings and being aware of how our behaviour and feelings can impact upon them are necessary aspects of forming and then sustaining positive relationships.

This topic focuses upon the need for children to articulate the range of feelings that they experience and to be able to distinguish between feelings which are comfortable and those which are uncomfortable. Recognising when a situation or person is the cause of uncomfortable feelings can allow for the development of self-management strategies.

Learning Objectives

- To identify feelings that people commonly experience.
- To promote an understanding of how their own behaviour and feelings can impact upon others.
- To distinguish between comfortable and uncomfortable feelings.
- To recognise the need to enlist the support of others.

Discussion

In a circle time session ask the children to identify as many different feelings as they can and list these on the board. Discuss how some feelings may be more comfortable than others, for example happiness, excitement and so on, whilst others tend to be uncomfortable, such as sadness or fear. Highlight the feelings with two coloured felt pens – perhaps red for uncomfortable feelings and yellow for comfortable feelings. Ask the children to describe two situations, one which made them feel happy and one which made them feel sad. Brainstorm lists of adjectives which describe how people look when they are feeling happy, sad, angry or afraid and ask the children if they may have ever made someone feel like this.

Using the Activity Pages

How Do We Feel?
The children could make use of safety mirrors and practise making angry, sad and happy faces prior to the drawing activity. Also, prompt them to consider a range of situations/experiences which might lead to these particular feelings and highlight any similarities/differences, for example all children would probably feel angry if they were bullied or called names. Focus also on the fact that things which make us feel this way might produce the same reactions and feelings in others.

More Feelings
Ensure that children have an opportunity to think about these six feelings prior to completing the activity page and can identify situations which have caused them to experience these feelings. They will also need some time to discuss the distinction between comfortable and uncomfortable feelings. The notion of good/bad feelings is not particularly helpful; for example, anger is not always a bad feeling. If someone makes a racist attack upon you, then you are justified in feeling angry.

Focus on Anger
Reinforce that it is acceptable to feel angry – it is how we show and manage our anger that is of real importance. Discuss with the children the range of strategies which might be available to them (including school-based facilities and resources) and elicit their own personal ideas and methods. This may be an opportunity to highlight the school's behaviour management policy and playground policy.

Follow-up

- Ask the children to keep a feelings diary for a week, recording in pictures/labels/short sentences how they feel on each day. They can also try to identify how they may have made others feel each day.
- Brainstorm and formulate a series of class rules entitled 'How we can make each other feel happy'. Emphasise the consequences of our behaviour upon others.
- Ask children to create their own 'feelings cartoon characters' and to devise stories in the form of cartoon strips.

How Do We Feel?

- Look at the children's faces. Can you see how they are feeling?

_____   _____   _____

- Draw a picture of yourself in each box when you feel like this.

| angry | sad | happy |

- When do you make others feel like this? Complete the sentences.

I make others feel angry when _____

_____ .

I make others feel sad when _____

_____ .

I make others feel happy when _____

_____ .

More Feelings

- Look at the pictures. How do you think Ajay is feeling? Label each picture. The words in the Feelings List below will help you.

Ajay is feeling _____ .	Ajay is feeling _____ .	Ajay is feeling _____ .
Ajay is feeling _____ .	Ajay is feeling _____ .	Ajay is feeling _____ .

- Think about these feelings. Are they comfortable or uncomfortable? Put a tick in the box to say which you think they are.

Feelings List	**Comfortable**	**Uncomfortable**
Jealous	☐	☐
Happy	☐	☐
Loved	☐	☐
Sad	☐	☐
Scared	☐	☐
Pleased	☐	☐

NOW Can some feelings be comfortable and uncomfortable at the same time? Think about this and discuss it with a friend.

Focus on Anger

- When do you feel angry? Put a tick ✔ in the box if you think what is happening in each picture would make you feel angry.

having your ball taken ☐	being pushed out ☐	being teased ☐
being told off ☐	being bullied ☐	not being chosen ☐

- How can you help yourself? Who can help you when you feel angry? Work with a partner and discuss your ideas.

NOW Design a poster to help children not to hit out when they feel angry. There are some ideas in the Ideas Box to help you, but you can include your own ideas too.

Ideas Box	
don't hit out	take a deep breath
count to ten	find a friend
walk away	ignore it
hold your hands behind your back	find a teacher

ideas page

Friends

Introduction

It is clearly essential that all children are given the opportunity to explore the social and emotional skills which will enable them to develop and maintain positive relationships. Children need to be taught to listen to and empathise with others, to play and work co-operatively, to take turns and to share their skills, emotions and material benefits. They need to learn to identify and respect the differences and similarities between people.

The fact that family and friends should care for each other needs to be central to any teaching on friendship.

This topic asks children to identify the attributes of good friends and to distinguish between positive and negative behaviours within significant relationships. Taking turns and showing consideration for others is also emphasised.

Learning Objectives

- To identify the qualities of a good friend.
- To continue to develop awareness of how their behaviour and feelings can affect those around them.
- To understand the importance of showing care and respect for family and friends.
- To begin to distinguish between positive and negative behaviours within relationships.

Using the Activity Pages

A Friend Is ...
Allow children to work in pairs on this activity. If someone is being unfriendly or unkind they may like to consider the impact of such behaviour. How does someone feel if others do not share or take turns, or if they are left out of a particular game or activity? What do you think of others when they behave in this way?

Taking Turns
Turn-taking is not just a necessary skill for playing games. The children can discuss the consequences of not taking turns in a conversation, or in a shop. Define the concept of good manners and showing courtesy to others.

Caring and Sharing
Children need to understand how they can show care and appreciation for those around them. Highlight the differences in caring emotionally/physically/materially. Emphasise the importance of not only sharing material things, but also of sharing time, friends and ideas.

Discussion

Begin the discussion with a circle time session in which children focus on the question 'Who are our friends?'. The children could name two to three significant people. Responses could include members of their family, their immediate peer group, people who live near to them or family pets. What is it that others do and say which lets you know that they are a good friend? Ask the children to focus on this question in groups and allow three to four minutes for them to nominate one child to report back to the rest of the class. Responses may include sharing toys, sweets and games, having similar interests, likes and dislikes, helping you. Use their responses to formulate a list of friendship characteristics.

Follow-up

- Stress the importance of not lashing out at friends when they annoy us. Read *Name Calling* by Itah Sadu to reinforce this.
- Ask the children to explain verbally how to play a turn-taking game and the rules for playing the game. Children could work in pairs on this activity, then present the explanation and role-play how to play the game to the rest of the class.
- Create a whole class book entitled 'People Who Care For Us'. The children could produce one page each detailing a significant/important person who cares for them and the caring behaviour that is shown to the children, for example parent, carer, step-parent, doctor, lunchtime supervisor, friend and so on.

A Friend Is ...

- Who is being a good friend? Put a tick ✓ or a cross ✗ inside each box, then give your reasons.

I think _____

_____

I think _____

_____

I think _____

_____

I think _____

_____

NOW List your friends who:
- are in your class
- are in your family
- are grown-up
- are animals/pets.

Taking Turns

- What are these people taking turns to do? Complete the sentences.

Paula and Sara are taking turns to _____.

Emma and Ash are taking turns to _____.

Lee and Ann are taking turns to _____.

The children are taking turns to _____.

- Draw yourself taking turns with others.

I am taking turns to _____.

Caring and Sharing

- Kayleigh cares for her friends and family. She also shares with them.

- Think of two people you can care for. Draw and label them.

- Think of two people you can share with. Draw and label them.

NOW Tell your teacher/tell your friend about the people who care for you.

ideas page

Making Rules

Introduction

Children need to learn that rules are important as they will help to keep them safe and healthy. They need to begin to appreciate that rules designed to protect the individual and safeguard society exist in a variety of contexts and situations, for example in friendships and relationships, in the classroom, within the local community and to protect the environment. The children should be provided with opportunities to agree and follow rules for their classroom and to understand how these rules will be of benefit to them.

This topic focuses upon the need to develop and make use of appropriate rules in a variety of contexts and situations. It aims to help children to see that following rules will be of benefit to them.

Learning Objectives

- To formulate a list of friendship rules.
- To label behaviours that are appropriate for the classroom.
- To distinguish between pro-social and anti-social behaviours.

Discussion

Make use of this discussion time either to reinforce existing classroom/school/playground rules or to enable children to understand the rules and to ensure a sense of ownership. Ask children to consider what would happen if they broke their classroom rules. What would it be like in the classroom?

Consider how and when people break rules outside the school environment. Provide picture examples from newspapers, magazines and books which illustrate a range of anti-social or rule-breaking behaviours. Ask the children to work in groups and focus on each picture. What is happening? What is wrong? How do the people concerned feel? What is the rule that is being broken and what should be done to put things right? The children could report their ideas to the whole class and the teacher could highlight the most positive and appropriate responses.

Using the Activity Pages

Friendship Rules
Read the friendship rules to the children prior to asking them to complete the activity page. Do they think these are good rules? Why? Consider the importance of being able to forgive and make up with friends when there has been a problem. Children could role-play making an apology.

Class Rules
Refer back to the initial discussion and the agreed classroom rules – display the rules you made, and allow the children to copy them, write them in their own words or simply to illustrate them. What is important is that they can articulate their own class rules. You can't keep a rule if you're not sure what it is!

Society's Rules
Allow children to discuss their ideas and to consider who is and who isn't keeping the rules. We need rules to keep us all safe. What do they think being 'safe' actually means? How do these rules help towards achieving that end?

Follow-up

- Reinforce the importance of treating each other with respect by reading from appropriate children's literature such as *Sweet Under Your Seat* by Tiffany Leeson.
- The children could create 'What would happen if I …?' cards which detail a positive or negative behaviour on one side of the card and the positive and negative outcomes on the reverse.
- Invite the local community police officer into the classroom to talk to the children about his or her role and to highlight the laws/rules that people need to obey and the reasons why they should do this. Children could prepare a range of relevant interview questions prior to the visit.

Friendship Rules

- What makes a good friend? Look at the friendship rules below. Connect them to the pictures with arrows.

Friendship Rules

Good friends take turns.

Good friends work together.

Good friends listen.

Good friends have fun.

Good friends help.

Good friends share.

NOW What makes a bad friend?
Talk about this and list your ideas.

© Belair (copiable page)   LESSON BANK – PSHE and Citizenship 1

Class Rules

- These are Cameron's class rules.

  * We keep our room tidy.
  * We take turns.
  * We listen to our teacher.
  * We do not shout or rush around the classroom.
  * We put up our hands.
  * We help each other.

- List your class rules.

  _____
  _____
  _____
  _____
  _____
  _____
  _____
  _____
  _____

NOW What happens if children break the rules? Discuss with a friend.

Society's Rules

- The people in the pictures are not thinking about other people. What rules are they breaking?

Do not _____

Do not _____

Do not _____

Do not _____

Do not _____

Do not _____

How do you think these rules keep us safe?
Talk about this with a friend.

ideas page

My World and Your World

Introduction

In terms of preparing to play an active role as citizens, children need to be taught that they belong to various groups and communities such as family and school. It is vital that they are encouraged to respect both the differences and similarities between people and to begin to identify the kinds of problems that will result if people choose not to respond to each other in a positive way.

This topic encourages the children to identify and label the different worlds they inhabit and to begin to consider how other children's lives may be different to their own. They are also asked to consider their own learning environment and to identify ways of making it better for all who need to use it.

Learning Objectives

- To appreciate how other children's lives may be different to their own.
- To understand the importance of respecting the differences and similarities between their worlds and those of others.
- To consider the consequences of not respecting and valuing difference.
- To consider their own learning environment and to identify changes which they could make to improve it.

Discussion

Ask the children in groups to consider the range of worlds that they belong to or currently inhabit. They could consider their homes, streets, towns, schools, religious institutions, families abroad, their country, their world and the universe. Prompt them to consider the concepts of environments and worlds and to see these as being both personal/private and as communal/public. Ask the children to feed back their ideas to the rest of the class. Highlight the range of worlds that they inhabit, reinforcing the continuum of 'small world' to 'large world'.

Focus on the children's own knowledge of other children's worlds. What do they know about children's lives in other parts of the globe? Emphasise the importance of valuing and respecting everyone's world – whether it is very different or very similar to your own.

Using the Activity Pages

Different Worlds
List on the board the vocabulary for the various possible worlds that might be within the children's experience. Ensure that the children identify both the 'smaller' and 'larger' worlds. Discuss how they should behave in each context and if each world has similar rules.

A Pen Pal
Provide the children with key words/spellings as appropriate. Collect a range of reference books/materials which show the class how children live and work in other parts of the world. Allow some time for discussion and for children to investigate these materials. Would they like to live in another country and experience going to school there? Which one would they choose? Why?

Things to Change
Draw a large plan of the classroom on a flip-chart so as to provide children with an example of how to go about this activity. Encourage the children to consider every individual's needs when planning the room. Do people like a quiet space/a special reading area? What else? Survey what each child would like to change as a result of this activity.

Follow-up

- Create a class display of 'Children of the World'.
- Ask a range of religious leaders to come into the classroom to talk to the children about their worlds, such as their beliefs, values and customs.
- Read *Dinosaurs and All That Rubbish* by Michael Foreman and *Where the Forest Meets the Sea* by Jeannie Baker in order to reinforce the importance of taking care of our worlds.

Different Worlds

- Look at Meena's different worlds.

| home | town | worship | school |

my world

- Draw and label your worlds.

My _____	My _____
My _____	My _____

NOW Look at a friend's worlds. Are they the same or different? How?

A Pen Pal

- Here is a pen pal!

Hello! My name is Lise.

I go to school in Cape Town as I live in South Africa. We all wear white clothes to school.

We swim in the sea for P.E. and we work hard at writing. What do you do?

Tell me!

From Lise

- Write back to Lise! (Fill in the spaces.)

Dear Lise,

Hello! My name is _____.

I go to school in _____.

I wear _____ to school.

We do _____ for P.E. and we work hard at _____.

Please write back!

From _____

Airmail
Par Avion

To

Lise Adjei
243A Pretoria Drive
Wulbick
Cape Town
CZ400IZ
South Africa

Things to Change

- Draw and label a plan of your classroom.
  These words will help you:

| shelf | door | book corner | desks/tables | toys | computer |
| window | painting area | carpet | board | pens | pencils |

NOW What would you like to change? What would make it a better classroom?

- On another sheet of paper draw and label what you think would be a better classroom.
- Why would this be better? Talk it over with a friend.

ideas page

Responsible Jobs

Introduction

Children should be given the opportunity to help others and to realise how they can play an active role in their family and community. The kind of roles and the level of responsibility given to them by parents and carers may vary considerably. Teachers will consequently need to be aware of these differences and encourage the children to value the range of jobs that others hold.

This topic identifies a range of jobs which the children can do in order to help others while emphasising the distinction between safe and unsafe jobs and behaviours. They are also encouraged to consider the roles of the various people who have responsible jobs within the community.

Learning Objectives

- To identify the roles of those who help them in a variety of contexts.
- To identify ways to help and be aware of how this affects those around them.
- To show care and respect for others.
- To know which jobs they can do safely themselves.

Discussion

Ask the children to identify all the people who help them both in school and in the community. In groups discuss what would result if these people suddenly decided not to help any more. Provide each group with one particular job to consider, for example teacher, refuse collector, road sweeper, school cleaner and so on. What would happen? How would they feel about it?

Next, focus on the kinds of jobs that the children can do at home and at school. Highlight any jobs which might not be safe, for example frying food, using the oven, washing windows and so on. Children could work in groups to identify two lists: safe jobs and unsafe jobs, and could nominate one group member to report their ideas to the rest of the class.

Using the Activity Pages

Home Jobs and School Jobs
Support the children with the vocabulary and words/phrases that they may need. Encourage the children to discuss the safety aspects or considerations for each job. Why do they need adult supervision when making a sandwich or washing up? What could happen? What are the 'safety rules' for these activities?

People Who Help Us
Allow the children to identify the people who have these responsible jobs. Allow time also for a small group discussion about the final activity. Highlight the importance of not enlisting support from strangers.

Is It Safe?
Discuss the pictures: 'I think this is safe/unsafe because …'. Reinforce particularly how all household products, including medicines, can be harmful if not used properly. The children could work in pairs to discuss their explanations.

Follow-up

- Create a wall display of the children's illustrations of 'safe jobs'.
- Collect and display a range of warning signs from magazines and catalogues. The children could create collages using these signs and explain why and when these signs are necessary.
- Invite the local fire prevention officer into the classroom to talk to the children about his or her job. The children can prepare questions prior to the visit and if possible video the conversation for future reference.

Home Jobs and School Jobs

- What can you do to help at home and at school?

HOME	SCHOOL
I can _____.	I can _____.
I can _____.	I can _____.
I can _____.	I can _____.
I can _____.	I can _____.

© Belair (copiable page)   LESSON BANK – PSHE and Citizenship 1

People Who Help Us

- Who will help? Draw an arrow to each picture and label the people who help us.

firefighter

police officer

teacher

paramedic

vet

A _____ helps us.

A _____ helps us.

A _____ helps us.

A _____ helps us.

A _____ helps us.

NOW What would you do if you got lost? Make a list/draw your ideas.

26 LESSON BANK – PSHE and Citizenship 1 © Belair (copiable page)

Is It Safe?

- Look at the pictures below. Are the children doing safe or unsafe things? Put a tick ✔ if you think something is safe. Put a cross ✗ if you think something is unsafe.

NOW Explain your answers.

ideas page

My Body

Introduction

Children of this age need to be taught how to start to make the choices which will ensure and improve their health and well-being. Being able to name the main parts of their bodies and to understand how to keep each part clean, fit and healthy is central to this process. They should also be encouraged to begin to distinguish between healthy and unhealthy options, both in terms of the food they eat and the exercise they take.

Children also need to be taught the basic rules for keeping safe in a variety of everyday contexts and in situations where they may be at risk of physical and emotional abuse. Saying 'no' and ways of doing so effectively need to be reinforced in order for the children to stay safe.

Learning Objectives

- To identify and label the parts of the body.
- To distinguish between unhealthy and healthy diets.
- To understand what keeping fit entails.
- To understand the importance of maintaining personal hygiene in order to control the spread of some diseases and to ensure social acceptability.

Discussion

Introduce the concept of 'our bodies' by singing the song 'Heads, shoulders, knees and toes' with the children, employing the appropriate pointing actions. Consider the importance of looking after our bodies by keeping them clean. In groups, ask the children what else they can do in order to keep their bodies fit and healthy. Consider the following: exercises you could do, foods you should eat and things you should avoid, how to keep your teeth healthy. The children could also consider who else could help them to stay fit and well, such as the doctor, gym instructor, swimming teacher and so on.

Finally, have a circle time session which focuses on keeping safe – on the road, in school, in the park and elsewhere. Emphasise the importance of saying 'no' to things that make you feel uncomfortable and eliciting the support of those you can trust.

Using the Activity Pages

Parts of the Body
Encourage the children to identify and label the body parts verbally prior to recording.

Keeping Healthy
Emphasise that kicking around a football, taking a short walk or helping to clean the car/house are all forms of exercise. Reinforce the importance of hygiene; for example, sneezing over someone spreads germs and disease. Point out that you can eat sugar, fats and salts as part of a healthy diet, but that making your whole diet consist of such foods will result in ill health. Children in particular need fat in their diets and they should be encouraged not to see it as a 'bad' thing.

Keeping Safe
Allow the children to work in pairs to share their ideas. How would they cross the road? Who would they go to for help if they were offered sweets by a stranger? Highlight the ways in which germs are spread via dirty hands and open rubbish tips.

Follow-up

- Show the children pictures of healthy and unhealthy teeth and diagrams which illustrate how and why decay can and does occur. The children can design leaflets to illustrate how to take care of their teeth.
- Complete a survey of 'Our favourite games and sports' and make use of ICT/block graphs/pictographs to illustrate the statistics.
- Reinforce the importance of saying 'no' to strangers and situations which make the children feel uncomfortable.

Parts of the Body

- This is me!
  Label the parts of the body. The list of words will help you.

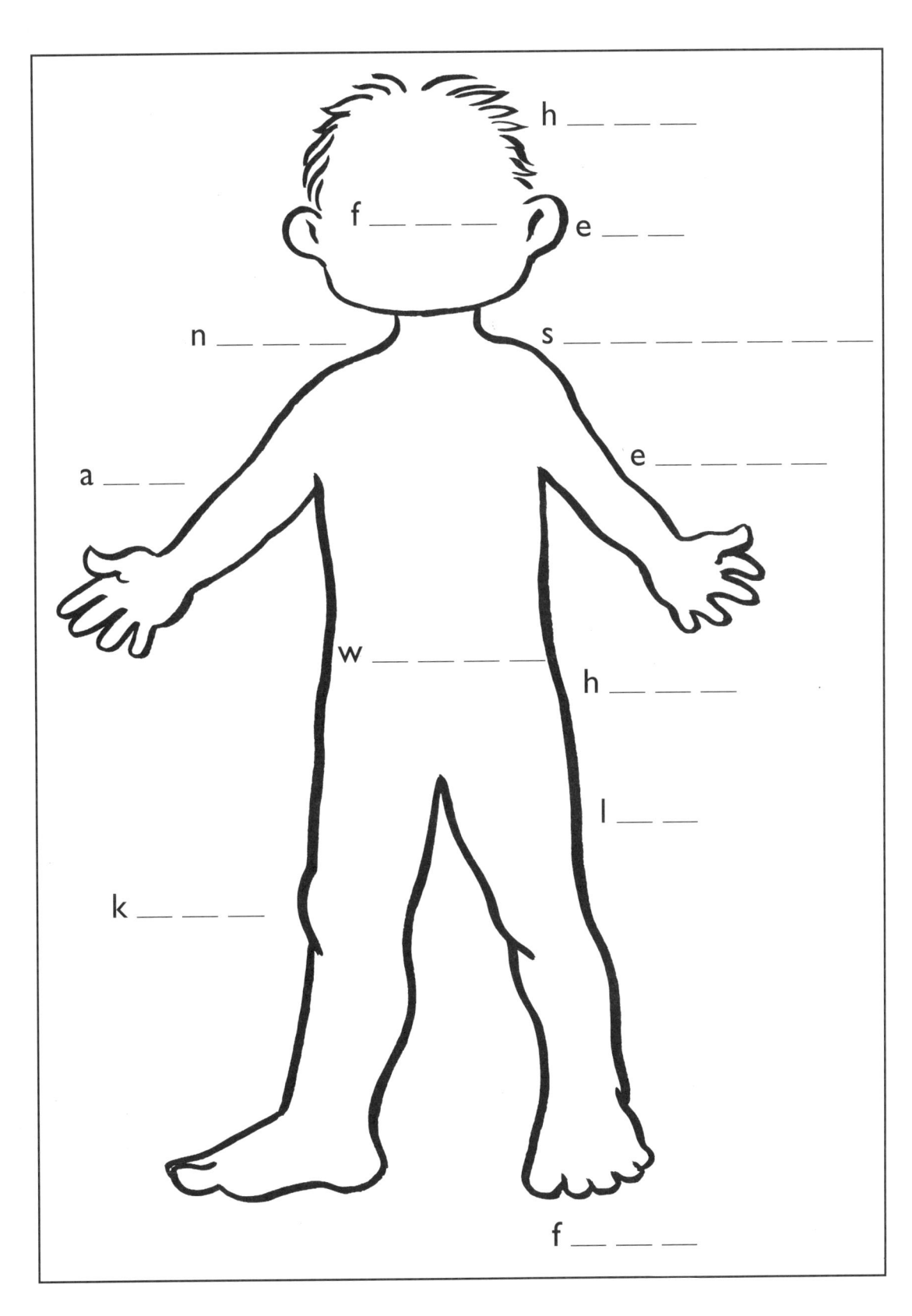

h _ _ _
f _ _ _ _
e _ _ _
n _ _ _ _
s _ _ _ _ _ _ _ _
a _ _ _
e _ _ _ _ _
w _ _ _ _ _
h _ _ _ _
l _ _ _
k _ _ _ _
f _ _ _ _

waist
face
hand
knee
neck
arm
foot
head
elbow
shoulder
leg
ear

Keeping Healthy

- Look at the pictures below. Are the children doing healthy or unhealthy things? Put a tick ✔ if you think something is healthy. Put a cross ✘ if you think something is unhealthy.

NOW Explain your answers.

Keeping Safe

- These children are not keeping safe.
  Explain what you think they should do to keep safe.

NOW How would you keep safe in **a)** the kitchen, and **b)** the bathroom? Write/draw your ideas.

ideas page

Caring for Others

Introduction

Developing and maintaining positive relationships is a two-way process of giving and receiving. Children at this stage need to learn to move from the more egocentric stage of early childhood to one in which they begin to identify the feelings and needs of others. The fact that they belong to various groups and communities and have varying responsibilities towards these needs to be reinforced, alongside the practical ways that they can show care for others. They need to learn how to co-operate with others and understand how their behaviour can affect those around them.

Learning Objectives

- To consider the ways in which they can show support for their friends and family.
- To distinguish between ways to help that are safe and practical and those that are not.
- To increase their ability to empathise with others.

Discussion

Encourage the children to spend some time thinking about who they love, value and care for and their reasons for doing so: 'I care for ... because ...'. Next, focus on how they show that they care for these people. What do they do in practical terms? Do they help parents with shopping/housework/cleaning the car? Do they help their friends with work/sorting out problems in the playground? Do they help their teachers by listening, behaving sensibly and working hard? The children could discuss their ideas in groups and make a list of caring dos and don'ts, for example: we care for our friends and family by listening to them; we don't care for them by ignoring their views and feelings; we care for our street by not dropping litter and not making a lot of noise.

Using the Activity Pages

Family
Be aware of cultural differences and the ways in which responsibilities and showing emotions/caring behaviours may vary. Encourage children to share their ideas and reinforce the importance of respecting and valuing differences.

Friends
Reinforce the definitions of a friend and the ways in which friends should behave. Identifying practical ways of caring for friends is a useful exercise.

Community
Allow children to work in pairs on the activity page so that they can discuss their ideas, listen to each other and learn the importance of being able to justify their own views. Caring for the community involves caring for others who live within it and for the buildings, streets and vegetation that make up the local environment.

Follow-up

- Create a portrait gallery of 'People We Care For'. The children could paint portraits or create a collage of portraits using photos/drawings/paintings of the people that they care for. Include family, friends, people in school and people who live both near and far.
- Reinforce the importance of thinking of other people's feelings and caring for their situations and well-being by reading *Gorilla* by Anthony Browne.
- Design illustrated charts to detail things that children can do in order to help others in the wider community.

Family

- Who is helping these people? Use arrows to match the pictures.

Explain how each person is being helpful.
How do you help people in your family?

Friends

- Jack is a good friend. He cares for his friends. Look at the pictures and match the sentences from the Sentence Box.

Sentence Box		
shares his sweets	shares his toys	looks after his friend
helps with work	listens to his friend	takes turns

Jack _____ .

Jack _____ .

Jack _____ .

Jack _____ .

Jack _____ .

Jack _____ .

NOW Write or draw about how you care for your friends.

34   LESSON BANK – PSHE and Citizenship 1   © Belair (copiable page)

Community

- Some people show that they care about their community. Some do not.

- Mark those that care with a blue X.
- Mark those that do not care with a red X.

NOW Explain your answers. Discuss them with a friend.

© Belair (copiable page)   LESSON BANK – PSHE and Citizenship 1   35

ideas page

Solving Problems

Introduction

Children need to be encouraged to take responsibility for their actions and to realise that negative behaviour on their part may result in other people taking negative action towards them. Learning how to distinguish between right and wrong and pro-social and anti-social behaviour alongside developing simple problem-solving strategies should enable them to maintain more positive relationships.

Learning how to cope effectively with bullying in particular needs to be emphasised and children should be taught that there are different types of teasing and bullying, and that bullying is wrong. They need to be shown where they can obtain help to deal with problems such as bullying.

Learning Objectives

- To identify solutions to everyday problems that they may observe or encounter in their local communities.
- To label and identify bullying behaviours.
- To know who can help them to deal with bullying.
- To understand that they are responsible for their own actions.

Discussion

Ask the children to identify a range of problems (without mentioning names) that they commonly experience or have observed in the playground. Once a list has been drawn up, split the class into smaller groups and allocate one of these playground problems to each group in the form of a question – for example, if someone is being bullied, what should they do? Where can they get help? If the older children won't let the younger ones play football, what can they do? How can this problem be sorted out? Emphasise the importance of co-operating and working together in order to find solutions to such problems. Ask one child from each group to feed back their answers to the class. Finally, ask children to identify specific home problems, such as with siblings who annoy them. Discuss positive ways of reacting.

Using the Activity Pages

A Playground Problem
Read through the mini-story with the children and refer them back to the initial discussion. Encourage them to discuss their strategies: ask a friend for help, stick up for yourself, find a teacher, fight back and so on. Which is the best strategy and why? Which is the worst and why? Children should articulate the consequences of each solution before completing the picture story. Focus on the importance of enlisting adult support.

Problems at Home
Allow time for the children to discuss these problems. Encourage them to describe what's going on in each picture and to identify the feelings of everyone concerned. What does Dad feel? How can you tell? (Body language, facial expression.) What does Ella feel? The last activity could be a whole class discussion. Focus also on ways of showing that you are sorry, such as taking actions to repair any damage.

Care in the Community
There are many social problems which the children, at this stage, could make no contribution towards redressing. However, it is important to be able to identify those who can help to find solutions, such as police officers, social workers and so on. Encourage an ethos of caring as opposed to making any stereotypical judgements of others, such as 'Tramps are all drunks and shouldn't be helped anyway'.

Follow-up

- Reinforce the importance of not accepting bullying behaviours both in and out of school. Read *Mr Gumpy's Outing* by John Burningham for the children to discuss.
- Encourage children in small groups to role-play problems and then to attempt to devise and role-play the solution.

A Playground Problem

- Look at the problem. What can the children do?

1. The children are playing football.

2. Two big boys take the ball.

3. The children are upset and angry.

- Draw and write what you think the children should do.

4.

4. _____

NOW Write about or draw a playground problem that has happened to you or you have seen.
What happened? How did the problem get sorted out?

Problems at Home

- Look at the problem in each picture. What should these people do? Draw and write your solutions.

Ella should _____

_____

Dad, Sam and James should _____

_____

NOW When do we need to say sorry? Why?
Write or draw a list.

LESSON BANK – PSHE and Citizenship 1

Care in the Community

- What do these people or animals need? Who can care for them and sort out the problem? Use arrows to match the pictures.

Look at three of the pictures and write about how you think the people were helping.

© Belair (copiable page)   LESSON BANK – PSHE and Citizenship 1   39

ideas page

Caring for Our Environments

Introduction

In preparing to play an active role as citizens, children need to be taught what improves and what harms their local, natural and built environments. Money from the government is allocated for services to maintain positive environments for people, and the children should be made aware of this fact. The children can discuss where they think money needs to be spent in order both to provide essential services such as refuse collection and to improve the quality of life in their environments.

This topic requires children to identify what needs to be cared for in their own environments, to consider the safety aspects of maintaining a litter-free environment and to plan and design an all-purpose play park.

Learning Objectives

- To label the parts of the school that need to be cared for and to understand who takes on such responsibilities.
- To consider the needs of others in planning and designing a play park.
- To understand what harms their local environment.
- To understand that money from government is allocated to providing services which maintain and ensure a good, clean and safe environment.

Discussion

Ask the children who helps to keep our environment clean and healthy. What do they do? How do they do it? Explain to the class where the money actually comes from to pay for these services. They might like to consider what they would spend some of the money on if they were provided with such an opportunity. Would they create car-free zones, special play parks, a butterfly park, leisure centres and so on? Ask them to justify their choices and to ensure that they take into account all the various needs of everyone in the community – not just their own.

Using the Activity Pages

Our School
Children need to develop their observation skills and to be aware of what's going on around them. Talk about how people help them to function within a positive environment, for example school cleaners, caretaker, gardener, kitchen staff and so on. They could also consider people who work in the background such as the school governors and the PTA. Ask the children how they can support this work. What can they do if they see a problem or recognise that something is not as it should be? How can they contribute? Allow children to discuss this in smaller groups.

Plan a Play Park
Talk the children through the example on the page and ask them to identify why Matt may have included these things. Who was he thinking of? Has he forgotten to consider the needs of any particular group?

Rubbish Everywhere
Allow time for discussion so that children can articulate why certain rubbish is not safe to handle. Reinforce safety rules.

Follow-up

- Reinforce the importance of caring for all the environments we live in by reading *The World that Jack Built* by Ruth Brown and *Dinosaurs and All That Rubbish* by Michael Foreman.
- Make up 'Tidy Tips' charts for the classroom, the bedroom/playroom, the street, the town/village. The children can record their ideas on strips of card in both pictures and writing.
- Create a 'Wonderful World Book'. Each child can contribute a page on which they detail (in words and pictures) one thing that would make the world a wonderful place for everyone to live in.

Our School

- Who helps to care for your school?

[Illustration labeled: cleaner, secretary, caretaker, cooks, gardener]

The _____ mends things and locks up the school.

The _____ keeps the school clean and tidy.

The _____ cuts the grass.

The _____ make our dinners.

The _____ answers the phone and types letters.

NOW Think about how you can help each of these people to do their job. Write down your ideas. Who else helps to care for your school?

Plan a Play Park

- This is Matt's dream play park.

My Play Park has:

A heated paddling pool
A sun house with books
A tree house
Ropes on the trees
Candy floss stall
An ice cream shop
An indoor games room

- Plan your own dream play park!

My Play Park

NOW Explain your ideas. Have you considered everyone's needs?

Rubbish Everywhere

- Paul is helping with his class and teacher in the park.
- Help him to decide if this rubbish is safe to pick up and put in a bin. Use arrows to show which rubbish is safe to pick up.

flowers	syringe	fish and chips
cigarette packet	pen	empty purse
dog mess	old boots	old books
newspaper	plastic bottle	old kettle
glass	old coat	paint pot

NOW Make a list of the rubbish that it would not be safe to pick up. Who could help you with this rubbish?

© Belair (copiable page)   LESSON BANK – PSHE and Citizenship 1   43

ideas page

Look to the Future

Introduction

Children need to be given the confidence by both adults and peers to enable them to begin to develop into responsible citizens who are able to make the most of their abilities. This topic therefore focuses upon the identification and labelling of current skills and future goals and aspirations. The children are given the opportunity to set personal targets and encouraged to consider wider world issues and problems and to understand how they can take some responsibility for the process of identifying necessary changes.

Learning Objectives

- To consider their strengths and skills and recognise what they are good at.
- To reflect upon past experiences and to understand the importance of learning from mistakes.
- To set realistic and achievable future targets.

Discussion

Discuss the notion of a good citizen being someone who cares for others and their environment. Ask the children in groups to make lists of the characteristics of a good citizen. What do good citizens actually do? How do they help others? How do they show that they are responsible? Highlight any similarities and differences in their views and ensure that all children have a clear understanding of what a good citizen is.

The children could try to identify each other's skills as part of a 'Compliments Circle Time' and proceed to identify changes they'd like to make in themselves. They could consider how they would set about trying to make these changes and who they could enlist to help them.

Using the Activity Pages

I Will Be ...
The children could refer back to the circle time discussion. It is obviously too early for the children to make decisions about what their future career should be, but most of them will probably have ideas of what they would like to be when they grow up. This activity encourages them to think of several options. They should be given a realistic idea of what a job actually entails – for example, being a police officer doesn't just involve capturing thieves, it also involves routine work. Encourage them to consider how doing their job well would benefit others.

A Better Place
Discuss the picture as a class prior to asking the children to complete the activity page. What is wrong? Why? What would they like to change? How does this picture make them feel? The children could try to identify either a global or a more immediate environmental problem that they would like to see changed.

Setting Personal Targets
Encourage the children to work independently on this task and to approach it with an appropriate degree of honesty – for example, if you know you need to share more/behave better in class/learn your spellings, then say so rather than try to ignore these facts! Reinforce that no one is expected to meet their targets without help. Identify a list of all the people who can support the children.

Follow-up

- Reinforce the concept of being a good citizen and caring for our environment by reading *Where the Forest Meets the Sea* by Jeannie Baker.
- Reinforce the importance of always making positive comments on the qualities children value in their classmates. Good friends will always try to build up your self-esteem and help you to progress in all areas. Read *Alex and Roy* by Mary Dickinson, *Michael* by Tony Bradman and *Amazing Grace* by Mary Hoffman to illustrate this.
- Make zigzag books which illustrate children's past, present and future. Make use of photographs and drawings to create a picture of how each child has progressed and to identify future aspirations, targets and desires.

I Will Be ...

- Think of some jobs that you might like to do when you grow up. Draw and label yourself doing them.

electrician   firefighter
dentist

When I grow up I might be a
_____.

teacher   refuse collector
doctor

When I grow up I might be a
_____.

computer programmer
shop assistant   accountant

When I grow up I might be a
_____.

NOW Explain your choices. Why would you like to do these jobs?

© Belair (copiable page)   LESSON BANK – PSHE and Citizenship 1

A Better Place

- Look at the picture below. What would you like to change? What would you like to add? Cross out what you would like to change.

- Make a list of what you would like to add.

_____

_____

_____

_____

_____

46   LESSON BANK – PSHE and Citizenship 1   © Belair (copiable page)

Setting Personal Targets

- Tick ✔ the boxes to show what you would like to do even better next year.

writing	singing	drawing	science
numbers	painting	being a good friend	keeping fit
helping others	my behaviour	homework	spellings
listening	sharing	the computer	tidying up

- Choose three targets to work on:

    My first target is _____ .

    My second target is _____ .

    My third target is _____ .

Useful Websites and Agencies

> The internet is constantly changing and so are the sites that appear on it. We cannot guarantee therefore that all these sites will still be active. At the time of going to press the sites were checked for their content. It is advisable, however, to check sites first yourself before children have access to them.

WEBSITES
- **Institute for Citizenship** – www.citizen.org.uk
- **Education World** – Curriculum/training: Teaching Citizenship's Five Themes – www.education-world.com/a_curr/curr008.shtml
- **Teaching children skills for conflict** – www.frognet.net/~apjn/library.htm
- **Philosophy for children and the teaching of thinking and teaching methods in citizenship** – www.waseda.ac.jp/intl-ac/bulletin/c04-05.html
- **Teaching children's rights** – www.socialstudies.org/resources/infoservices/CHARACTEREDUCATION.html
- **Teaching citizenship** – www.socialstudies.org/resources/infoservices/CITIZENSHIP.html
- **Education for citizenship and the teaching of democracy** – www.qca.org.uk/citizenship_summary.htm
- **BBC** – www.bbc.co.uk/education/bully
- **ChildLine** – www.childline.org.uk
- **Peer support systems in schools** – www.mentalhealth.org.uk/peer/forum.htm
- **Interactivity safety education centre (Bournemouth)** – www.streetwise.org.uk

AGENCIES
- **Antidote,** 5th floor, 45 Beech Street, London EC2Y 8AD. Tel 020 7588 5151 (This organisation promotes the development of emotional literacy in children – publications, conferences, seminars.)
- **British Epilepsy Association,** Anstey House, 40 Hanover Square, Leeds LS3 1BE. Tel (helpline) 0808 800 5050
- **Child Accident Prevention Trust,** 4th floor, 18–20 Farringdon Lane, London EC1R 3HA. Tel 020 7608 3828
- **Diabetes UK,** 10 Queen Anne Street, London W1M 0BD. Tel 020 7323 1531
- **Family Planning Association,** 2–12 Pentonville Road, London N1 9FP. Tel 020 7837 4044
- **Guide** (health, social and disability information). Tel 01452 331131
- **Health Information Matters,** 231 Queensway, Milton Keynes. Tel 01908 631030
- **National Asthma Campaign,** Providence House, Providence Place, London N1 0NT. Tel (general) 020 7226 2260; (helpline for medical advice) 0845 701 0203
- **National Eczema Association,** 163 Eversholt Street, London NW1 1BU. Tel (information line) 0870 241 3604
- **NHS Direct** (health information). Tel 0845 4647
- **ROSPA** (Royal Society for the Prevention of Accidents), The Information Centre, 353 Bristol Road, Birmingham B5 7ST. Tel 0121 248 2000
- **TACADE** (Teachers' Advisory Council on Alcohol and Drug Education), 1 Hulme Place, The Crescent, Salford M5 4QA. Tel 0161 745 8925